MAKE MONEY ONLINE: EFFICIENT STRATEGIES TO MAKE MONEY ONLINE WITH ADSENSE, CLICKBANK AND AFFILIATE MARKETING

TOM JACKSON

TABLE OF CONTENTS

WHY I WROTE THIS BOOK

I wrote this book because I wanted to reach out to more people and tell them that in the new century there are new and creative ways to make money with the internet. For instance affiliate marketing can get very profitable over time. I hope the reader will get to action and put the wisdom in this book into practice.

WHY YOU SHOULD READ THIS BOOK

This book will help you to gain financial freedom through multiple streams of income. If you put some amount of work in these streams you will get a massive amount of passive income over time.

Adsense is for everybody When Google's AdSense appeared, there happen to be plenty of men and women that doubted Google's thought will be marketable and truly develop any earnings. Nevertheless as we stand right here in recent times It might be almost definitely the most popular shell out for each simply click enterprise in the world. Without a doubt, all People nay sayers wound up ingesting their unique words and phrases and phrases in the long run. And that is as the people at Google hardly ever go and do a little something with out evaluating whether or not Will probably be prosperous, or notably how worthwhile it truly is. But clearly, as you could extremely properly know, AdSense is don't just worthwhile for Google. It is usually profitable for the folks who advertise by means of AdWords and very valuable for publishers who utilize it to create earnings which are occasionally just terrific. So 1 must talk to himself why This really is these kind of a very good deal for everyone. Plus the worry in on your own could be very justified since you rarely come across a point which is successful for everyone with the chain. So why would AdSense be any exceptional. Thoroughly, AdSense is exactly where it stands now, supplying Rewards for everyone in the sport since it exploits a spot in the net's marketing and advertising products. The thing is, the online world is an extremely interactive atmosphere, and its interactions originate within the individuals who uncover on their own browsing. They decide on if to comply with a selected backlink together with the time period "navigating" could be most likely essentially the most exact only one at describing this scenario. So AdSense is great largely since it backlinks with each other likely consumers and sellers. Certainly, You'll want to hand it out to Google for a superb principle. They know you will find Adult males and ladies on the market that have to get things and other people who would like to sell them the factors they're eager on. And Google AdSense can help consumers in the 2 styles receive one another. It seriously works for that site readers, as the product is rather clear. You don't see an enormous graphic banner which tries to entice you into getting another thing. You simply see a couple of phrases. And after you like What ever you see you'll be able to just click it. It works just because men and women have not got that feeling of someone wishing to lure them into shelling out profits. Ironically, On the flip side, they're Faulty. It definitely functions to your AdWords advertisers due to truth their adverts go Nearly almost everywhere. Not simply just will they attain by themselves outlined in Google's seek out which is able to get gazillions of hits per day, up entrance without Performing just as much for Search engine optimization and prepared Substantially. Their commercials can achieve any World-wide-web-website that promotions with anything at all comparable to what ever They are making an attempt to deliver. Now you need to recognize They might below no situation pull of these good promotion by on their own. Which brings us on the factor that makes Google's AdSense a publisher's best friend. It emanates from The truth that the advertisements are contextual, they in some way connected to the search term phrases you cope with on your web site webpage. Simply because folks or on your World wide web web-site, which specials with a certain subject, you already know they're pondering that material. But, hey, keep out a instant, Google appreciates some organizations which choose to promote your site website visitors a bit a little something connected with their subject matter. Google wishes your company, you desire Google's advertisers and the web site site visitors just will need to acquire things. And that's the essence of what will make AdSense a great provide for everybody. This really is certainly most likely one of the most financially rewarding hook-up give you're at any time planning to see wherever on the internet. So you've to appreciate Google for acknowledging a killer deal. You've got to know how correctly thought out, but standard this program genuinely is. Absolutely sure, in workout it's obtained a number of quirks but All People are compact and, up up to now Anybody is apparently savoring Google's AdSense.

ADSENSE – POSITIVE ASPECTS AND DRAWBACKS

Ch You have got that Online website on-line for rather some time, its producing an amazing range of hits on a daily basis in addition to you might be thinking about whether or not to use AdSense advertising on it to really make it make some kind of cash circulation. Properly This is usually an define from the advantages and disadvantages in the method of Earth-large-World wide web promoting. AdSense has certainly strike the net like nearly anything from One more Earth and people are certainly excited about it all over the place. You are going to learn unfavorable things to Adsense and possibilities to contemplate. AdSense is normally an excellent Source for webmasters. Whilst, they'd use to bother with ways to carry sufficient bucks to help keep their sites rewarding, or no less than preserve them on-line Individuals anxieties are absent. AdSense permits internet site house owners to forget about All Those people worries and concentrate on building top-quality content for their Internet sites. In reality, the emphasis is currently on developing good quality content material (normally connected to the most effective-shelling out terms and phrases) that can provide you lots of site guests. AdSense may also extremely properly designed-in with your website, It is actually very very easily customizable With regards to colors, measurement and place which suggests you may experiment with it in Just about any way you prefer To optimize your earnings. AdSense is a very good implies of creating a relentless revenue on your Online internet site. All you will need to do is generate some high-quality content and retain it up to date frequently and you may just about Remain off your internet site. An excessive amount of customers are endeavor just that presently with AdSense, so It is actually change into form of a corporation in by itself. It is also a marvelous strategy simply because you could have the exact same account advertising on all your web pages. This is undoubtedly ideal for web-site proprietors wit plenty of articles since it signifies they don't have to produce Plenty of accounts unnecessarily. But as pointed out, previously mentioned, there are plenty of destructive sides to advertising and marketing and advertising with AdSense and This is slightly list of this type of Negatives. Evidently the largest detrimental result the Ad-Sense computer software may have on you is thru Google closing your accounts. Normally this will come about on account of so identified as 'just click on fraud', which indicates any person can be creating synthetic clicks on your own webpage. There is certainly surely just one significantly nasty side to that. It doesn't have to typically be you earning These synthetic clicks. It could pretty properly be your Competitiveness carrying out this as a way to shut you down, or perhaps the competitor of whoever is promoting all by yourself Web content, trying to get to vacation their advertising and marketing and advertising expenses up. The earning AdSense supplies you happen to be under no instances Regular. The truth is, they aren't even in the vicinity of to that. Absolutely anything you need to do for your World-wide-web web page could end up remaining a significant miscalculation costing you a considerable degree of dollars. It is admittedly that kind of pressure that includes a negative influence on you. To start with off, you continually would like to confirm your site is while in the Emphasize of search engines like google and yahoo like google and yahoo when Adult men and girls are searching for irrespective of what it really is your website is about. For those who tumble limited to do this you won't have any website readers, and that not shockingly signifies you won't have any Ad-Sense cash flow. In a means This may be nothing in any respect new, as any sort of making revenue on the net with advertising has this kind of drawback. And finally, A further key difficulty is you constantly really want to feed your internet site with higher and increased written content. Now, needless to say, specified Web-sites are certainly beautifully geared in direction of carrying out this but which has a couple of sorts of material this is quite hard to realize. This is usually why the remedies of the copywriter are employed to deliver Progressively more information. When crafting distinctive content, the smartest thing a web site proprietor can do is analyze a topic thoroughly after which return to crafting with a lot of information they might out in their very own private words and phrases, and Show their very own specific feeling on. So you will find the benefits and drawbacks of utilizing the AdSense Neighborhood for developing earnings Through advertising. Now the selection of whether these be just good for you is yours.

ACQUIRING LIKELY WITH ADSENSE

A significant element In the quickly adoption of AdSense is normally that it's been really easy for publishers to find the ads on their own web site as speedily while you quite possibly can. Integrating AdSense as part of your Site can take only a couple of minutes, and you'll be on your own way with several effectively designed-in AdSense ads. The incredibly initial thing It's important to do is navigate to http://www.google.com/adsense And perhaps make use of or log in in conjunction with your present account and password. What follows will likely be a Web content presenting the Google AdSense Stipulations which you should conform to in order to move forward. You will be offered by using a report Web site web site which you can use to obtain an in depth standing on how your AdSense marketing is endeavor. This allows you to improve your World-wide-web website's contents and structure To improve your AdSense earnings. On the best of 1's site you even have website link in your set up part in which you'll be able to make the code that would should be pasted on your internet site as a way to have AdSense banners with all your webpage. You may employ AdSense for text (the stated adverts), employing a lookup box or with referrals. Your determination One of the these choices is dependent on how individuals will navigate your site. In the long run, There exists a "My Account" tab which lets you Construct specifics relating to your account, payment and tax details. To include a textual content advert in your Web-site, return for the "AdSense Set up" tab and click on the "AdSense for content articles" hyperlink. Be sure you might have cookies enabled during the browser. You can also make a desire in between advertisement styles and relationship versions. The former comprise textual articles and or illustrations or shots relating to a specific web site for each unit, most with an in depth description, the latter only contain back backlinks to specified varieties. Of course, It's really a little bit tricky to know which form you'll want to use so you must most likely experiment with equally for some time before you choose to make your thoughts up. You can even see an illustration of how the unit will lookup to The best of your respective respective site. However, It truly is probable you are going to only make use of a couple advert designs and one particular distinct Web site backlink unit on any presented webpage. Which is thought to be a go which Google needs For top of the range Manage. One more transfer is to make your mind up on your consist of construction and colours. You'll be able to fundamentally pick out any shade palette you find yourself selecting with Google presenting a couple of of its own if you don't have time or talent to make just one. You could potentially regularly watch how the palette will glimpse in the aid of the illustration. The one that actually works perfect regarding Visible charm and revenues will range Whilst using the lookup, genuinely sense and published information of a web internet site. Even so, your advert formats are restricted to a call of eleven formats. There is certainly an "Advert Formats" relationship which takes you to a Site that enables you to see all even of All those in motion as a way to make your mind up most effective which one satisfies your internet site. In some instances in essence probably the most intrusive, doesn't operate perfect nevertheless all once again, This could vary from Website to Site. Once you total with customization, you can click on "Commence" in the underside of your Site. You at the moment are presented with a piece entitled "AdSense for Prepared content material". It is possible to simply click wherever while in the textual articles Which reveals the JavaScript necessary to get AdSense Doing the job. This will promptly settle on the text In the box. You might then replicate it and paste it into your World-wide-web webpages right away.

Should you employ dynamic web pages, you need to paste this code in your template In order as a way that it receives exhibited on any Web-site of your website. Some advertisers choose to not Show Adsense on pretty much every single page, which is understandable. An illustration of This is usually a business which has adsense, may perhaps even perhaps have phrases and challenge which could inevitably provide lawful implies which might Nearly unquestionably be considered inappropriate. Precisely exactly what is then continue to remaining so as to do is get articles on the internet site (offered you did not have any by now). Google AdSense crawlers will Soon pay a visit to the Web page, making certain the commercials shown are applicable in your Site's product. So you are all concluded. For a simple page This could indeed be thought of a subject matter of a few minutes, which can be precisely what can make AdSense the option for many. Even though it is quick, its mass enchantment also will cause it being the best. Through remaining the most nicely-liked, advertisers and publishers alike see Adsense and Adwords as their natural in the beginning preference.

GOOGLE PPC – CONTENT ARTICLES OR LOOKUP?

When advertising and marketing and marketing with invest per click on Google delivers the advertiser two broad options. Marketing in search results, promoting in Websites content or unquestionably numerous prefer to do the two. Promoting in lookup implies that success are exhibited in Google beneath queries, and in its distributors search engine results. Google information promoting and internet marketing pertains to The individuals Internet sites who pick out to include "Adsense" into their Web-websites. As adsense quickly expands, it truly is at the moment viewable on quite a bit of internet sites through the Globe-broad-web. Nonetheless, quite a few advertisers are shunning this in favor of just internet marketing in search engine results. There are various explanations for this, plus the Original is believe in. This has lengthy been a results of lesser Website-internet sites, as a result of to adsense empires selecting to embark on Only click on Fraud. Despite the fact that this situation takes position in research it is far quite a bit much less dominant. People who dedicate Basically click on Fraud on investigation are These eager to weaken a competitor's ROI. With Adsense the similar applies, along with the Web content operator making an try and boost his revenues dealing with equivalent procedures. Another excuse why Web site proprietors are deciding upon to sector place out with product could be the enthusiasm on the customer when He's on a web website. Any individual that is with a Distinctive Website, besides the advertisers could quite possibly be there for fully various factors. One particular example is really a web site speaking about the disadvantages of Adsense, would actually return adverts for anyone providing "Adsense Internet sites" which include. Men and women could click on it, but These are definitely not likely to receive proper following reading through a negative evaluation. The opposite rationale could be that the individual across the adsense World wide website was in essence trying to find what is the best shade palette to employ. The person for that explanation would not Find the advert pertinent, but may well click the advert within a procedure Completely cost-free system. Adsense Web-sites will also be usually rejected from the advertiser since they really feel it needs further administration. Examining through Internet sites to Learn how correct These are, and modifying their bids To make sure they continue to appear to be on a Web-site. With a few words and phrases and phrases acquiring a Neighborhood of all-around five hundred Website-web-sites, it is unquestionably a laborous and dear task. Even though Here is your situation, various also see that their Adwords account returns Web sites, that don't even seem like trying to find that will help their crucial phrases. The occasion that is ripe, are People today marketing beneath authorized phrases who present up on adsense Websites "terms and conditions" and "privateness coverage" web pages. Although many are rejecting articles product promoting, there stay people who sense it provides exactly the same ROI to look. A reason for this can be found by in The reality that A growing number of advertisers are only determining on research. As this transpires the advertiser has less Amounts of Opposition so the expense of the phrase lowers. Advertisers are getting a great ROI from publisher's Internet sites who commit to actively endorse the advertiser's services within their written content. An example of This can be understood from when any individual is speaking about printing solutions, and truly ideal suggests the advertiser's services and products. This may be a optimistic change for equally the publisher along with the advertiser, and a good way for publishers to maneuver ahead. Despite this, publishers Even so have to remember, to not be much much too crystal clear in enterprise this, or savvy potential prospective buyers will definitely figure out the publisher's intention. Another rationale why advertisers are buying content is to increase their scale, nevertheless this can even be accomplished all over other search engines. The very fact obtaining said that on the other hand exists that those who select content advertising definitely really should decide on the Google Adsense Local community. It really is managed substantially and earlier pointed out yahoo's and a few Some others equivalents while its top rated-top quality community of publishers implies the advertisers will take full advantage of having the ability to distribute their info by a various assortment of World wide web websites. In spite of Adsense getting the best possible PPC information material distributor, it unquestionably doesn't Examine to search for the advertiser. On lookup the revenue possibilities are usually extra experienced, further managed, and less fraudulent. This has seen advertisers persistently pick investigate about material. Despite this advertiser's really really should generally check adsense and find out if it can provide the ROI they are searching for. Some advertisers assert that information offers a significantly better return for his or her tiny enterprise than exploration. This differs, Nevertheless usually lookup remains King for PPC advertisers.

HOW ADSENSE ALTERED THE NET ENTIRE WORLD

At any time as a result of simple fact Google arrived up Combined with the master idea which is AdSense, the world wide web has reworked in a number of suggests no one would have ever suspected. Many of these are definitely good adjustments Numerous Other folks are not. This can be a smaller exploration of how a fantastic advertising and marketing and advertising and marketing plan has taken the net by storm. It bargains Whilst utilizing the advancements advertisers and publishers and in addition World wide web website individuals have undergone Anytime given that AdSense has become a daily Portion of our on-line everyday living. Even prior to AdSense came out quite a bit of persons had been getting advertising by means of of AdWords. It ensured quite a lot of publicity By means of getting your Site outlined at the most beneficial in Google try to find queries. It took away lots of the agony and value of Web-site positioning and the massive stretch of time you experienced to attend correct until eventually you were past but not least on major. It developed launching an internet site, a simple procedure to instant profitability as a substitute to an enduring tactic without having possessing swift returns. From the usage of AdSense, the chance appeared of acquiring your adverts present up on just about any site on the web which includes absolutely anything that even resembles your enterprise is about. And so It is actually for that intent that AdSense has brought a fresh perception of promotion and promoting to the online sector put. Proper ahead of PPC improperly rated Sites needed to publicize offline to get any legitimate Original publicity. Organizations no much more need to seek out the providers of highly-priced experts to produce very elaborate marketing and advertising campaigns. There won't be any substantial charges of jogging your adverts on websites which It's important to Independently consider to search for. All you should do is visualize several major phrases for your organization, join with Google AdWords and Allow Google control the rest of the equation. Even though it wants daily administration automation saves considerable time for advertisers. Needless to say, more than likely the greatest alter in how the online entire world operates due to AdSense arises through the publishers' viewpoint. Whereas a single would Previously have to leap by way of several hoops to obtain an online web page to even help on your own now Adult men and women are earning fortunes off their internet sites. This contributes to inspiration for information product, and sources for Environment-wide-World-wide-web surfers. That typically normally signifies web site publishers have to worry a lot more specifics on what information lies on their own web site, and the general way their web pages seem as a substitute then be concerned with the economic specifics of keeping a internet site's profitability. Despite the fact that time is invested in adsense, a big revenue investment decision is just not. It actually is not any shock the blogging phenomenon exploded when AdSense arrived out a few many years ago. Any person could just make a web page a couple of matter he was enthusiastic about and earning a living out of it By means of AdSense. And thirdly, you can't ignore the consequences AdSense has expert in excessive from the casual on a daily basis Earth-huge-Website surfer. Whereas Adult males and girls accustomed not to even acknowledge banners solely (which psychologically is a really attention-grabbing element to observe) the precise predicament is completely various for textual information adverts. People currently should have a prolonged have a look at a sponsored advert. Why? Properly as your complete setup provides forth a sense of confidence with regards into the advertiser. Folks Will not ignore a textual content advert as extremely simply because they do a graphical banner. Yet another issue to note is The very fact graphical banners grew to become even much less financially rewarding nowadays. It's as a result of this that Lots of people are strolling away from affiliate range networks to AdSense. Surely, there are literally undesirable outcomes also, with persons producing Worldwide-web-web-sites completely for the intention of running AdSense on them and equally as completely, with a considerable phenomenon of 'click on fraud', Adult men and women building artificial clicks for different causes. But Google does look at to handle these actions, and seriously is simply not staying blamed for this kind of individuals' methods. All in all Google AdSense is reworking just how the web industry place performs and It might be doing so generally in a good way. Now These with Recommendations can generate them down, and get paid cash from them. All All those seeking to come across info can find it less challenging, and people trying to capture the attention of a client foundation can perform so within a particular way. Adsense has modified the Internet by way of supporting the financial passions of businesses, as well as the utility of customers.

SPECIFICALLY SIMPLY HOW MUCH CASH WILL I GENERATE BY MEANS OF ADSENSE?

If you're looking at Google's AdSense technique you will be surely inquiring yourself how much you could make from this type of method, and you also almost unquestionably Imagine You could not make up to it is feasible to from standard promoting techniques. Google, definitely, retains lots of secrecy pertaining to the quantity AdWords advertisers shell out out for every Every single click directed for their web page plus the similar applies for the quantity AdSense banner holders make from their Internet sites. While there's nothing official, rumors circulate all-about the net globe concerning the diploma of earnings a Website can get by making use of AdSense. And many people (illegally) disclose just how much These are creating with AdSense. You will find tales of oldsters elevating in extra of 1 thousand pounds every month making use of AdSense. Moreover, there are actually stories of oldsters exceeding $a single hundred,000.00 regular monthly nonetheless it's style of tough to consider a lot of these stories. The reality to the subject matter is usually that For those who have a little Internet site and you just want it to assist alone, and don't want to reach your pocket for its regime upkeep expenses you can easily probably do that with AdSense. AdSense is normally Great for those who host loads of webpages. Irrespective of whether the reported internet pages Actually Do not make a lot of web-site readers individually, Each and every and every click on counts and you might receive up with a lot of money by carrying out this. Which just goes to determine that from time to time amount issues Pretty much about leading high-quality. There is no telling simply how much dollars you are going to make by making use of Google's AdSense however , you may style of inform on your own, in advance of in truth setting up, by utilizing a handful of elements into account. Really first, is the level of visits you're going to get every single day. Nevertheless There is no Answer to estimate especially on this, you'll be able to commonly make a secure assumption that When you have loads of clicks every day You will be setting up good money. Also, This really is dependent on what precisely your Internet site is about. In case your Web-site is about every little thing perfectly-known (tunes, sex, what ever) you take place To make certain to acquire quite a lot of banner clicks. These Use a coefficient affiliated with them, generally known as the CTR (click as a result of ratio). Essentially, what it interprets to is that if a substantial proportion of your internet site's people click the advertisements You will be manufacturing more cash. And the best way to try this actually would be to very own some very well-preferred material with your Web web-site, ensuring the a person-way inbound links speedy consumers in course of recognized objects Similarly. Then needless to say, There exists unquestionably the situation and array of advertisements on your internet site. Even though you don't need to overdo it, obtaining A good number of one-way backlinks will certainly crank out much more revenue for you like a webmaster. Is not going to However feel that, that if You simply include tons of adverts in a very important aspect of your respective World wide web website, visitors could continually just skip them (and come to be particular that many do exactly that). There is a thing between an art in addition to a science to positioning your ads. Folks routinely look in specified sites and in no way look for in Other folks, and recognizing this an online web-site creator and/ or webmaster can execute an extreme volume of issues to improve his earnings with AdSense. All in all, the sum of cash you make with AdSense is dependent upon many things. But Should really there is a web site with intriguing contents and/or several internet pages, and if the detail can be a regularly sizeable range of focused people day-to-day, it is feasible to guess you'll be developing some huge cash with AdSense. Regardless of whether You're not in the above mentioned types, AdSense remains to be worthy of making use of for The rationale that there is little if any difficulties in natural environment it up, and repeatedly it could possibly support economically support the world wide web web page, Despite the fact that now becoming a superb bonus to have through the entire publish-up at the conclusion of the thirty day period.

POSITIONING OF ADVERTS

Right away right after using AdSense for quite a while you have to have begun to inquire your self if there is absolutely anything at all in the slightest degree you are able to do to improve your AdSense dependent earnings. But before choosing to go on experimenting with this and that setup You will need to know a handful of challenges about positioning. The first thing you need to know is that there is no typical posture that is unquestionably guaranteed to completely transform your earnings. That presently staying stated, the part Formerly outlined about experimenting is alleged to be taken pretty much. You must think about as numerous setups as you could potentially to discover The solution with the greatest revenue. But, clearly picked Places generally execute much improved then Several Other folks. Definitely, Google acknowledges this additionally they publish a "warmth map" of just the amount of earnings adverts put in chosen elements of the website can Express you. Experimenting is commonly the simplest way yow will find, what matches the sub acutely knowledgeable head of the viewers. Frequently Probably the most beneficial ads are positioned all through the Principal articles, Commonly suitable previously mentioned it. But This can be undoubtedly less than no instances a rule and there are numerous exceptions to it. Only one determined exception is acquiring a information internet web site or just about anything very similar to a very new website. If This genuinely is your circumstance, you may perhaps commonly discover that you choose to make a good deal more earnings by inserting your ads at The underside from the prepared content material, right right in advance of responses start out out. This is due to as individuals close studying a story, they have got a brief minute where They are hoping to find a thing much more to conduct. Plus your AdSense advertisements can give them that anything at all. Also, positioning commercials in the direction of the still left aspect of just one's Website appears to execute far improved Almost consistently. Not shockingly, This is certainly sensible for The key reason why that textual information is mostly published from left to suitable (Until you originate from precise nations specifically wherever It is one particular other way all-close to). Folks will end a sentence and return their eyes around the remaining posture, which implies they may have the next chance of recognizing your ads. Also, There exists a little bit far more to this then just proudly owning adverts visually in the right area. Must you have additional then only one ad You should hassle with the place by They are positioned in the code as well. And there is a very good motive behind this issue. AdSense fills the ads within the purchase it finds them in the offer. Which suggests that if the key insert you have acquired In the code isn't the just one making the very best earnings, you may ahead of very long begin to reduce cash, relatively then receive a lot more. This is because of if AdSense doesn't have any more adverts it may dietary complement your Area with common community supplier adverts or simply just disappear it blank completely. Meaning that, if you find yourself unfortunate, you may perhaps find yourself finding your most gratifying spots not getting any terrific ads during the slightest degree. To dietary health supplement your revenues There are other fears with the number of adverts you should put in your website. The trouble is The actual fact For anyone who has lots of, in its place then deliver much more income, you will have a lower click by price, as guests are inclined to not adjust to adverts in the areas particularly the place these come in excessive. You must frequently check how the customers interact with your web site. Keep a watch out for wherever the visitors will likely be looking at your internet web site most. This is normally the placement the place you intend to make use within your First adverts. Also think about not To place adverts in aggravating positions as that would assure a reduce just click on by fee. Not remarkably, You mostly require to obtain adverts that Mix in with your penned material and customarily Never make The client's existence on your site an disagreeable a single certain. The legitimate mystery is supplying an enjoyable working experience for the customer, While creating revenues from their exploration. And another time, inevitably the best income will probably be obtained Through many experimentation. You'll want to unquestionably use AdSense's channels factor and be about the watch out for how individual adverts as aspect within your Net internet pages are enterprise whilst altering the positions to increased supplement your earnings.

SEARCH ENGINE OPTIMIZATION FOR ADSENSE

When you've got been utilizing Google's AdSense on your web-pages you certainly seriously really feel the necessity to by some suggests crank out a great deal more qualified people for your web site, which consequently would translate to supplemental Ad-Sense click and a better earnings. But who does one Do this? Properly, An important way you will get web site guests to check out your Site (other then making use of AdWords, which transpires to be inspired too) is to employ some approaches to acquire engines like google supply An increasing amount of customers towards your Website, by rating major in search results for your personal topics of fascination. Contrary to popular belief That could be a way, significantly greater usually generally known as research-engine optimization or merely Online search engine marketing. So here are plenty of recommendations that arrive handy beneath just about every beginner or Qualified optimizer's belt. The really initial thing you will need to handle is the actual offer code and construction of your respective web page. This should be saved as simple as possible. The trouble will occur when AdSense and the various search engines like google and yahoo them selves start to have problems in extracting very perhaps one of the most relevant look for phrases on your internet site as a result of a also elaborate construction. Next, Check out to obtain each of your webpages concentrate on only one specific matter. In this manner It can be really a large sum considerably less tough for them to obtain indexed adequately and to the AdSense adverts to normally be in keeping with the articles or blog posts of the net web page itself. Also, take into consideration not to include loads of hyperlinks as part of one's Website also. This also suggests you need to consider not to operate with plenty of AdSense ads along with your webpage probably. If there are literally chosen research phrases you desire to to focus on, be sure the term you would like to focus on is existing in the title, in the key paragraphs and Within the title around the file. As you're at it it really is a good idea to make certain the time period springs up while in the location's very last paragraphs. Not to mention, It is really essential for your individual facts to get reliable and strong published articles. How will you Do that? Correctly the easiest way to do it is to search out another thing you transpire to generally be definitely enthusiastic about. In this manner, supplying you with give it loads of labor you may be sure to have an exquisite website page quite quickly. Should the content material you hire in your website is in the general public place (which is highly discouraged) Make certain that you no less than give it an First title, and insert a gap as well as a closing paragraph within your extremely possess. This requires a short while, but when, instantly after All set, you still are not able to encounter your website page near to the very best, you must try out rewriting your title furthermore your very first and previous paragraphs. It will never choose Substantially, normally just transforming A few terms gives you the very best good results. And of, process you'll find the use of search term resources that can support you find some fantastic vital phrases to include on the site that can push visitors in your Site An ever-increasing variety of. So Those individuals are about The basic strategies in search engine optimisation. Yow will learn lots of Pc program products to assist you in carrying out this, as well as, Google is an excellent place to search for this. In the end, you can find that Seo is a complex subject matter, and entire guides have currently been composed on The subject also. You may encounter that you have a lot of optimization You should do in an effort to obtain a expanding range of Web page website visitors for your World-wide-web web site and clicking People today useful AdSense banners.

MEANS FOR ADSENSE

In the event you be just boarding about the AdSense observe, and looking to Find a swift way to generate the gains you have witnessed all keeping pulled of all online, you might be interested in a handful of means. These application software sources are meant to help AdSense publishers in obtaining a exceptional information on how traffic flows Through their internet internet site. Some will allow you to in comprehension which keywords and phrases and phrases obtain you more money and which locations Offer you the greatest AdSense payment. The simplest this kind of programs obtainable is AdSense Gold (http://www.profitbooks.com/go/astracker) which helps you to have an enhanced expertise in which adverts and formats in essence get extra clicks and which can be helpful or virtually ineffective. This plan capabilities by monitoring sights and clicks on the various publisher's pages. It even goes in terms of providing you the probability to determine which referrer Almost each visitor arrived in by. There exists a Definitely cost-free tool recognized as SynSense (http://www.singerscreations.com/RSS/Posts/235.asp) which may be far more of an AdSense checking Source. This sits whilst inside the tray and provides actualized AdSense stats while you hover your mouse about its icon. It can be an exceptionally magnificent Device for people which would like to be educated on how their AdSense is executing all of the time inside the day. Google will give you stats in the csv construction on their Site. So someone designed a Computer software which will routinely acquire these kinds of data files and extract a lot of information from them. The title with the Gadget is CSV AdStats and it is actually obtainable from http://www.nix.fr/en/csvadstats.aspx?q=download It's obtained lots of capabilities, such as the probability to very personalize pointed out stats, exporting aspects and charts to other formats. It can be in French although the language can incredibly very conveniently be improved to English. Evidently any Resource can only obtain these stats as routinely as 15 minutes nevertheless the authors are really very well conscious of that reality and none of People instruments will get you in challenges with Google because of that. If, However, you might be browsing material usually, and also your Source of possibility will be the Firefox Net browser, you can find an extension for this process that permits you to point of view the stats within your placement bar. Yet again, this software is mindful of Google's fifteen moment rule and enforces its use, quarter-hour remaining the bare least time amongst updates. The Google AdSense notifier for Firefox is often received from http://code.mincus.com/?p=3 There's unquestionably also a software referred to as Golden Keyword phrases accessible which will help you in acquiring The perfect keywords on your Web web site. It can be truly productive and really consumer friendly. It does involve a providing selling price tag nevertheless, it costs $forty nine.ninety five and it would be attained from http://www.regnow.com/softsell/nph-softsell.cgi?item=8616-2 In order it is possible to determine, software method builders are earning An ever-increasing amount of programs meant to assist you within your quest To improve your AdSense cash flow. But before you plan to head out attempting to find them Remember that Google has quite a few alternatives of its personal Moreover. It does offer some opinions (albeit a bit extra constrained) and utilizing the 'channels' attribute is an effective way of getting out which adverts on your own Web-site are literally bringing in the majority of the revenue. Be throughout the watch out as new means seem to be day-to-day and assure to invest time in your site, as that is the genuine essential in achievements with AdSense.

CLICKBANK IS ABOUT SIGNIFICANTLY GREATER THAN MERELY THE THINGS

Virtually all us consider Clickbank similar to a assistance focused totally to digital solutions and solutions. A electronic product by definition will likely be a a little something you present. It would be an e-reserve about almost everything from child's tales to an Investigation of scientific despair to your guidebook to how one can Participate in a marvelous recreation of golf. It would turn into a application offer which makes life span less complicated or a extremely great recreation you invented. But by definition, it is definitely "one thing". Which means that in that context, Clickbank is concerning the things. One of ClickBank's laws of residing for suppliers strains up Together with the solutions only means of the Market because you are anticipated to supply the merchandise in 24 hrs of payment and if possible right away by obtain. The tactic of delivery may possibly quite possibly vary. It might be by obtain, by e-mail or by directing The shopper into a membership website to get the products or services. Clickbank doesn't go into the primary details given that The shopper can get his goods and services inside of more than enough time window. When The selection of predicts which can be made available from the Clickbank Current market is unlimited, Clickbank doesn't have any provision for providing qualified products and services implementing their great marketplace machines. That 24 hour rule which can be fully realistic for any digital product or service is basically problematic if the nature of your respective Net business enterprise is actually a aid you present, irrespective of whether the end result is really an product. A firm is distributed according to an abundance of variables which the service provider can't often dictate. Some options are continual with periodic payments maybe dependant upon milestones or on deliverables. In both case, a specified shipping and delivery working day is questionable as well as to limit that timeframe to 24 hrs Just about out with the condition. A great number of retailers have discovered tips on how to reap the benefits of the wonderful Market infrastructure along with the merchant account businesses of Clickbank to carry out tiny business with purchasers that functionality in the 24 hour solution shipping and delivery and shipping and delivery restriction. An awesome example is ghostwriting. A shopper will get in contact which has a merchant implementing ClickBank's discussion resources for making arrangements to the development of the number of content articles or weblog posts. But the particular "merchandise" wouldn't be set up all through the Clickbank merchandising program till the products and solutions is whole and well prepared for offer. Then The shopper and buy the merchandise which occurs for being an final result to the companies and use Clickbank's systems to work Along with the ghostwriter. Regardless of no matter whether you organize your services for being moved by Clickbank ahead of time or Any time you extensive the support, The vital ingredient is for the price to have perfectly comprehended appropriate prior to logging the undertaking into Clickbank. This can be healthful for your enterprise romance among seller and purchaser and retains your nose thoroughly clean with Clickbank also. It might take into account some purpose to transform your hourly billed company right into a set selling price tag products. But merely focus on the final result. Thus for anyone who is employed through the hour to supply a stipulations doc to get a undertaking, you can set the fixed rate if The task is near the cease and you simply arrange the payment car as a Clickbank digital companies.

Also Try to remember The truth that Clickbank expects to take a look at shipping and delivery. Your organization could have consisted of the number of fifteen phone cellphone calls where you offer Professional steering and progress as section of the subject matter of experience. So to create a deliverable, keep the notes for each session and get ready a summary at the very best that captures the consequences of your sessions Besides your conclusions and you could possibly "sell" that in direction of your shopper for the price of the full consulting costs Together with the fifteen lessons. It significantly just demands some creativeness and talent to not just Contemplate exterior the house the box to work in the Clickbank box to offer your services and products as being a digital product or service. But as an online entrepreneur, turning out to be progressive is second character to you personally.

BARE MINIMUM OVERHEAD – MOST GROSS SALES

There's an out-of-date phrase about technological know-how that goes "If it ain't broke, Hardly ever resolve it". That basic theory may perhaps pretty effectively be legitimate of one of many Numerous fantastic attributes about the Clickbank marketplace and how they founded you up to put Option into their marketplaces. When you want to sector in Clickbank, the method is quite simple. You establish an account like you need to do on any other Internet site. And there is a $fifty Expense to become a sound vendor to provide solutions with the Clickbank affiliate membership. But when you consider that Clickbank has more than one hundred fifty,000 affiliate marketers ready to pick up your electronic solution and provide it and that numerous of these types of affiliate marketers are most of the most completed On-line Entrepreneurs in cyberspace, you will be probably gonna make that $fifty back again within the 1st Alternative to the procedure. A slip-up some new services provider make is to find a Clickbank account as just one goods account. So in order to put quite a few goods out in on the technique, the idea is you require quite a few dozen accounts. This just isn't the Clickbank functioning philosophy. They want you To place just as much goods as is reasonable for the procedure so All people today would make lots of cash flow. In almost any circumstance, not simply do the affiliate marketers create profits on Each and each sale, you prosper and Clickbank usually takes just a bit Payment simultaneously. That those small commissions incorporate approximately massive bucks for your those who run this really large Market. They know they're not intending to get prosperous on Men and women $fifty commence expenditures. The reality that Clickbank by plan encourages you to offer numerous products with just one account Construct is mirrored in the way by which your account is structured. It is possible to offer nearly fifty digital solutions and methods on Clickbank and do all of it under only one account. This provides you the chance to select whole good thing about your $fifty program price (which signifies $one for every products or services being marketed if you take complete good thing about Clickbank). But Additionally it is much easier to regulate and the more items you offer underneath a person unique umbrella, the increased your rating in the Clickbank Marketplace may very well be. They are pretty persuasive motivations to put into practice an individual account to deal with your whole solutions offerings. To fully utilize Clickbank's sources to provide quite a few merchandise down below one account, you ought to system to organize the items and solutions to maneuver over the Clickbank landing internet site facility. The landing Web content is your house foundation with the product or service which the affiliates who seize your options and provide them across the net have to have to acquire to backlink their prospects toward your service or product. Now in previous instances Whilst Clickbank encourages you to advertise plenty of goods underneath 1 individual account, they only supported anyone landing Online page for each account. This problem is remaining labored out in just Clickbank but it has been a weak point within the Clickbank infrastructure genuinely value stopping. So to stage all over using Clickbank's landing Website entirely, basically arrange a landing web site for each merchandise beyond Clickbank. On this way you even have the many flexibleness on this planet to crank out that minimal Web site as elaborate as It's also advisable to to increase and modify it simply because you are doing this outside of the Clickbank system. Your solution income Web-site is neutral of the tactic so you might help it become component of your respective About-all Planet-huge-Website advertising and marketing software program which can integrate other methods to the net environment recent marketplace including MySpace and YouTube. You might uncover solutions Every single purchased commercially and in just Clickbank to intercept incoming targeted traffic for an merchandise and supply it about the landing web site you've got setup externally to current market the merchandise. But operate Together with the system so your affiliate Entrepreneurs hold the sale and so are energized to make further revenue so they lead to you to definitely successful. They're a bunch incredibly perfectly worthy of getting excellent treatment of.

FINDING PRODUCTS ON CLICKBANK

When you're environment oneself up remaining an affiliate on Clickbank, you Nearly expertise overload. Clickbank offers ten,000 items which you could potentially decide from to supply online, Nearly each and every of which typically provides a reasonably generous commission. The challenge is the way to go about acquiring just the proper methods to signify. You don't have to bother with the shops just because beneath the Clickbank system, it is achievable to decide on a product and promptly get started marketing it and Clickbank handles every single on the list of commissions and interaction with the merchant solely. The worry will come due to the fact there are literally just numerous products on Clickbank to pick from that you could potentially allow it to be a full-time endeavor assessing these merchandise. So developing a method to "drill down" into that significant catalog to products that not merely seem wise to be able to offer but That ought to depict utmost profitability to you personally is critical. It will probably become a procedure that may aid you slender down catalog of goods You will be excited about Together with a technique you could potentially refine and increase as you get a lot more common Really don't just Along with the Clickbank merchandise but Combined with the equipment they provide you To guage All All those things. The First And maybe ideal technique to "reduce with the herd" goods that could be just good for you as being a Clickbank affiliate is category. Clickbank has It actually is shops assign distinctive forms to each with the merchandise which are all through the industry. That way if You basically wish to provide adventure video game titles, you will see that class of items after which get much more unique about the particular objects that attract you. There is certainly two explanations course is going to be an enormous Examine of the achievements providing Clickbank products. Just one specific is you know your area of interest sector. You will just get these items to Your entire body of consumers you recognize beautifully. You understand their preferences and so they arrive at you to acquire goods and alternatives to fit their specific passions plus the realm of specialised know-how you share using your customer foundation. The 2nd rationale is that you know incredibly effectively what you like to provide and what you're superior at promoting. You could possibly Maybe flounder attempting to present self assistance courses in car mend but be truly excellent at providing ebooks about enterprise. And the greater you are able to Merge the methods you are going to offer as well as your certain market place in addition to your strategies and passions, the higher probability that you are very likely to give several models and make yourself together with the Clickbank merchant rich. In this way Most people wins. Making use of search phrase phrases the same as what your shoppers could use to Track down the products and solutions and remedies you might be delivering, you could trim down the selection of products to only those you would probably desire to market. But Clickbank will give you a prosperity of data that may be analyzed for making the decisions of which ones make the final word Slice. You could potentially sort the product document you've produced by level of popularity to understand which of Those people people merchandise is delivering properly for numerous affiliates on Clickbank by now. It would be very easy to want to select those which could be major sellers for plenty of affiliate marketers but use some judgment right here. Remember also that if lots of affiliate marketers have picked up Those people people methods, the Web may be saturated with offerings of that merchandise and you simply might have an excessive amount of Competition for promoting the similar Clickbank goods and services offering. Check out developments of gross product sales and see if you may find products that are soaring in attractiveness While not peaked Nevertheless. Individuals will likely be your cash makers. Amount of recognition is not the only variable that may issue you in the direction of Clickbank products and solutions that can deliver an awesome return on the effort and effort to offer them from Clickbank. Get Observe the Cost diploma. Similar to a rule only get products that current you which has a twenty 5% or bigger Payment. Which means the merchant truly really wants to share the prosperity with and you'll see a really balanced make the most of the income you make. Other variable constraints really really should be the service or product ought to have a % of whole sale of no fewer than 13 lbs or larger, a 70% or improved referral level, negligible return portions As well as a gravity of 50 or bigger. By obtaining an analysis method that combines all these variables concerning the merchandise under consideration, You will find a terrific prospect of selecting winners and cash makers inside the Clickbank merchandise library Any time.

EARNING CLICKBANK AFFILIATE ENTREPRENEURS

Your really individual Something lots of retailers enjoy about Inserting services or products out above the Clickbank sector is they definitely don't should recruit affiliate Entrepreneurs to provide the answer. Clickbank has some 100 and fifty,000 affiliate marketers scanning the item listings everyday and finding up new digital things to market. Among the this army are several of the best rated names in World wide web promoting who may perhaps really very well be investigating your goods and services and selecting it virtually offer for his or her really large consumer foundation. You must feel that with this particular great degree of affiliate marketers that you'll be specific some superb profits in the event you area pretty much any products all around. But Truth of the matter be told, It certainly is nevertheless feasible to record your Digital merchandise within the Clickbank Market place and for it to only "sit there". For something, your item is competing for thing to consider using a few ten,000 other goods. And the goods which already have robust income and good affiliate Affiliation are the ones which could be in superior need. Inside the party your products enters within a lifeless prevent, it's a not easy to route to amass it in to your "swiftly lane" so The great affiliate marketers take into consideration notice of it. Additionally, Amongst the These 100 and fifty,000 keen revenue folks nowadays, You'll find there's fantastic share of terrible varieties. And Whenever your product gets picked up by rookie affiliate marketers or These out there but who will be not knowledgeable at no matter what they are doing, your goods and services can just "lay there" earning you speculate what went Absolutely Improper. So anything at all can accomplish to draw affiliate marketers with your product or service and also to even recruit your specific affiliate marketers is completely justified to acquire your product sales shifting in Clickbank. Plenty of outlets keep on currently being glad to easily allow the character of Clickbank to deliver affiliate marketers their way. But to get powerful and really get on the market and appeal to affiliate marketers for yourself will provide you with some possession of the strategy. Not just would you increase your entire means of having thriving in the Clickbank surroundings, you acquire associations with affiliate marketers and work additional in partnership with recruited affiliate marketers than it is best to in case you simply relied fully on "random" affiliate Entrepreneurs selecting up your goods and starting to make the gains you demand. Pinpointing new affiliate marketers and developing them segment of one's respective affiliate network might take some Resourceful wondering but in some ways you have currently bought every one of the approaches you'll need at your disposal. Your Primary target is to create traces of communications which could not exist if you simply still left the Clickbank affiliate arrangement work as it's. The idea to the Clickbank Modern society is the fact that merchants and affiliates do top-quality if they don't have to speak simply because you are able to give attention to producing far more product or service and affiliate marketers can concentrate on product sales and not being compelled to generally be accountable to dozens of retailers Need to they be promoting several products. Undoubtedly, this components does function in a good amount of circumstances, appreciably If the product receives to get Portion of a catalog of a big variety of Countless solutions and remedies for the couple of rather major affiliate Entrepreneurs who shift many digital products under the Clickbank method. But that doesn't imply there exists not an abundance of location throughout the Clickbank technique in your partnership passionate romance in between affiliate and service company. You presently could extremely well be in this sort of relationships outside of Clickbank with affiliate marketers you're utilized with by way of your Site. That human system of gross gross sales individuals is really a all-natural location to go to recruit affiliate Entrepreneurs to offer to fit your requires in Clickbank. By approaching them to contemplate turning out to become Factor of Clickbank and presenting your merchandise there, you could sweeten the offer by presenting a larger commission furthermore the entice of this kind of a considerable catalog of products there they may become further prosperous advertising and marketing in the Clickbank Market place. The right problem is usually to cultivate a huge human entire body of affiliates, several of whom do encourage your goods and alternatives "anonymously" and People with whom that you are in romance. You have the ability to recruit affiliates for long run product or service bulletins and simply by thanking affiliate marketers who manufactured your former service or product presenting successful and supplying to keep up them during the loop if you set a lot extra products into your marketplace. By building a mailing listing of prosperous Clickbank affiliate Entrepreneurs who like your get The task completed and want to know When you've got something new to provide in Clickbank, you can bit by bit and slowly develop a "team" of income those with an outstanding consider your advertising and promotion method And how they may be Component of with all your achievements as currently being a merchant by in search of you out When you've got anything new to provide. More than one strategy to Prosperity on Clickbank As is real in almost any Market, the probable for revenue producing is many and frequently new inside a site where by merchants and shoppers are sometimes coming jointly to barter and make promotions happen. So being an entrepreneur it's a sensible plan to work with a deal with about the assorted methods to profitability in precisely what is the largest World wide web Market to the world - Clickbank. Clickbank at any specified time signifies more than ten,000 merchandise which any affiliate with the proper Clickbank account can endorse and provide. So by turning into an affiliate, that huge catalog is completely at your disposal to sell with no need to obtain so that you can ask for permission or any formality in anyway. This is the Clickbank agreement Using the sellers that's amongst the significant tricks to good results available in the market. Signing up to be an affiliate on Clickbank is shockingly simple and you could have an account. Basically log into clickbank.com and stage as a result of the method inside a come up with a distinction of moments. So you are willing to go. Now just keep on to your alternatives catalog and operate within the classes to locate the specialized specialized niche you prefer to to inspire and also the items which you happen to be sensation have the best prospective for income. Next to advertising and marketing as an affiliate, Inserting your unique items to the Clickbank Current market is A powerful suggests to produce major income. And setting up an item is nearly so simple as turning into an affiliate. Your support company account on Clickbank is really a a person time cost of $fifty which you are going to make once again speedily with regards to the sale of 1 merchandise that moves properly. And economic local weather of Clickbank could it be is feasible to promote fifty answers at a time through the identical account for that same organize cost. That you will be sure to make a minimum of $1 for each item to purchase again that setup Value. Once you get your merchandise prepare and several profits logged, You will find a armed service of close to one hundred fifty,000 marketers seriously to accumulate your product and get it in existence to the sale stream. That means that after you need to do The crucial make solutions, that you will be with the world wide web marketing and marketing recreation and you will hand off that minimal issues to experts who're proficient at providing in fact 1000s of products of 1's product or service. You don't have to do an element. Just established a Cost degree which takes place for being a proportion the affiliate can make for his effort and afterwards just sit once again and Permit that Armed forces of proficient On the internet Entrepreneurs do their matters. The cash can just roll in while you concentrate on making new Alternative. Obviously you will get proactive instead of foresee strangers to promote your Answer. If you have a product profits group, place them to work as Clickbank affiliates and they can concentration completely in your answers. Clickbank supplies their impressive Market construction and possibly the best run provider company accounts on-line to guarantee your cash is gathered and accounted for appropriately and safely and securely and securely and sent to you immediately. You will find other strategies to pick out up extra earnings as Clickbank benefits Pretty much any routines that Benefits the Market. In case you ship Clickbank consumers with the support by itself, that referral receives a reward. Additionally, you will come across specialty Clickbank advertising and marketing principles getting to be designed and promoted frequently like the Clickbank storefront. So retain the attention inside the Clickbank newsletters and "Exactly what is New?" Internet sites as it can be such A fast transferring Market that you decide on to may well find a brand new moneymaking opportunity available Organized that you ought to leap into and pull Nonetheless a lot far more revenue your way by using Clickbank.

HARMLESS AND SEEM PROMOTING ON CLICKBANK

Inside the non-Planet-huge-Net ecosystem, retailers are frequently battling a war with shoplifters and folk who'd think about your items without purchasing it. You'd almost certainly think that this sort of point would not become a problem in an online based surroundings. But in Clickbank that is the most important On the web marketplace on earth, amongst the best challenges is halting people from downloading a digital item and then not future By the use of with payment. Like every other retail environment you will discover stability weaknesses in Clickbank as you can find with any software program system atmosphere. But with some excellent warning on the Portion of The seller at the person stage, you may discover ways to plug Folks stability holes and keep the Option safe so when it will get downloaded, you receives a commission. In actual fact we in some cases are our quite individual worst enemies after we transform Clickbank retailers simply because we conduct some things that undermine the safety Clickbank now has put in place. The first thing to acknowledge everytime you present-day sector on Clickbank is the fact that It truly is off limits to put backlinks toward your goods info on Clickbank on somebody within just your other Internet site webpages. Don't attempt to prolong the advertising and marketing and advertising by driving visitors to your Clickbank Web content in this fashion. For ideal safety, the sole true way your shoppers must have the chance to down load your product or service is adhering to beneath-likely the normal Clickbank payment webpages which implement that payment is made just in advance of delivery and shipping. This can be certainly 1 very simple precaution to keep up anyone from attending towards your information and bypassing the payment approach. Yet one more excellent trigger not To place back again links on your solution as part of your World wide web website is always that it's going to result in this again once again door with your products to search on the main search engines as a person-way one-way links Many others can use. Google will begin to see the inbound links and index them and they may glance reasonably substantial in online search engine rankings and that's really perilous for the security of your respective Remedy. Some threats that the answer Site webpage could get leaked are beyond your Command. You will find On the net burglars who'd accumulate your thanks webpage and product or service URL anywhere and short article them on newsgroups and discussion boards devoted to underground theft of on-line merchandise. The actual volume of thefts You may have from that taking place is sort of little. The particular difficulty is if People postings get picked up and in depth on the web search engine. Then you certainly definately could have a serious security risk. There exists someone transfer that could dispose of the online search engine trouble which takes place to become The larger sized danger in your thanks or products web pages for Clickbank obtaining "available on the market". That is without a doubt to Get hold of the Webhosting corporation. They've got a method while in the server diploma to build a customized safety file which is checked by the main search engines like yahoo to exclude sure knowledge data files form turning into indexed. By incorporating the URL for your products and solutions web page on Clickbank together with your thanks Web content, whether or not People today back backlinks get outlined, you quit the bleeding as being a alternative so the quantity of losses will probably be pretty minimal. Nonetheless this Resolution should be utilised with Extreme warning. The file that many Web-site hosting servers utilized is referred to as the robots.txt file. The trouble is hackers are quite mindful of that file around serps like google are. And each time a hacker can recognize that file, and they're able to, that opens the doorway to your destinations within your solution paperwork to typically be stolen and after that posted on A further Internet site which opens The entire can of worms all all once more. The smartest point is never to reference All People locations within the least Thus if there'll very likely be any leakage in their spot, It will most likely be by means of hackers whose have an affect on is minimal at best. Like that no below you reside a completely thoroughly clean existence and undertaking Everything it is possible to. And by looking at the Clickbank FAQ and updates notices so you're going to be often up-to-date on any new security updates They are really establishing.

GIVING EVERY DAY ON CLICKBANK

There is a prevailing mythology regarding the Clickbank market-place that it's almost an exertion and hard work free of charge earnings system. Its quick to locate the Completely wrong strategy since it is in fact a Marketplace where must you Get the goods in existence to the Clickbank Market, there are actually earlier mentioned 100 and fifty,000 keen affiliate Entrepreneurs willing to pick up your services or products and begin to offer it. Persons affiliate marketers don't must Enable you to understand that they're going to supply your merchandise or Obtain your authorization. Just by virtue of at the moment remaining with the Clickbank Group offers them liberty to market your merchandise. So in idea you might potentially location an item to select from and see its earnings soar without the need of getting far more effort and effort than that. But Even when you will get some marginal or great profits from a solutions working with that technique, you don't want to simply accept marginal or remarkable. You should get quite possibly the most money possible you could from your listings on Clickbank. And Which means you don't just industry sooner or later and location your solution on car pilot. You give daily on Clickbank so you encounter the benefits regarding bigger gross income, bigger income as well as a increased position simply because you are now being extreme about your earnings. And Any time your items rise inside the item income figures, they get noticed by simpler affiliate marketers in Clickbank and you will get to a larger viewers. It is about building momentum after which holding it. A person strategy to increase your revenue within the goods has additional to perform with generation than it does advertising. Do you have to have the answer you set in existence so You are not advertising and marketing Yet another man or woman's items, just one hundred% of Whatsoever you have from Clickbank after the affiliate Slice and Clickbank's fees are yours. It is achievable to equally maintain the answer made for yourself and buy the legal rights to it Unquestionably or permit it to get by your self. An amazing illustration of This system is through the marketing and promotion of an e-book. Just in case you compose it fully you, you have total ownership in excess of it and each among the revenue are yours. But even Should you do have a killer system for an e e book that should market like hot-cakes, not all of us are writers. But there are literally starving artists in existence on the web undertaking firms who to the couple hundred pounds will place with one another an e e-book that could go through perfectly and deliver an excellent notion in your purchasers. And by acquiring the reserve ghostwritten, you purchase in depth ownership from your legal legal rights with the e ebook and you'll market it and experience all the advantages all your self. Inside Clickbank, you'll find a prosperity of sources you could use to aid hold tabs You should not just on how properly your things are likely but around the connection of endorsing to item movement And precisely how your commissions glance To be sure They are really healthy as an alternative to going through any type of Fee theft that is often attainable in Clickbank. So Percentage of delivering on a daily basis isn't really a great deal just being attentive to money but toward the variables of solution sales including the achievement of certain affiliates and the level your Answer is achieving to generally be a fascinating product or service to promote. There exists a detail to be spelled out for simple positioning and Getting that may help your product or service move up so extra affiliate marketers opt for it up. So Once you Get the goods in towards the process, ensure it is A crucial ambition to amass mindful of a lot of the Clickbank tracking and reporting equipment. These reviews can Help you to stay along with your Answer's usefulness each day and when you see transform transpiring, you could control appropriately. That may be the type of dynamic goods administration that may carry about far more robust gross income. If the thing is your merchandise have a change inside the figures that is not healthful, you've got acquired the prospect to intervene and make modifications Or even pull the goods if it's a major ample scenario. On the other hand, if you see a sudden surge in attractiveness and products income and A much bigger participation Within the product, you are able to do your portion to be sure the affiliate Entrepreneurs are enabled to jump over the band wagon and make your merchandise prosperous. And although the refined changes to the way you area your items and contend with internet marketing is just not exactly marketing daily, it might be making solution income perform increased for yourself every single day and also the final result of higher income is equivalent.

ACQUIRING CLICKBANK TO THE NEXT PHASE

The make any difference that is unquestionably so great for you When you signal on to acquire an affiliate in Clickbank is likewise the issue which could be so troublesome concerning the market-place and that's how enormous it certainly is. With in extra of 10,000 items accessible for you to definitely market, just the endeavor of getting all of them after which you'll be able to picking out and organizing them, generally is a genuine trouble. And For individuals who have wrestled with tips on how to get equally as much Clickbank solution before your consumers and Nonetheless continue to keep an orderly plan it is feasible to accomplish The task with together with your buyers can use, a little bit aid goes a terrific distance. Just like quite a bit of marketing requires whilst, Clickbank has a method to assist you kick your administration of the massive Clickbank catalog to a special amount of money. The source they provide you would probably be the Clickbank Mall which occurs to get a Useful resource You could have for gratis that is definitely a great way to Arrange product or service. It may be a large Enrich in your gross product sales and profitability Moreover. There are literally far more earnings becoming created making use of the Clickbank Shopping center and advertising and advertising the Clickbank things using the mall principle. So this one particular unique unique Instrument can create numerous streams of cash flow for yourself basically executing

That which you presently do effectively, promotion products on Clickbank. Simply because You should use the Clickbank Shopping mall system to prepare the upper things on Clickbank into comprehensible types, you be certain it's plenty fewer complicated with the buyers to find the problems they would want to buy through you. The opportunity for commissions results in currently being fairly important as lots of Clickbank affiliates have famous all around 75% commissions and a chance to marketplace A huge number of Clickbank products due to organizational energy Together with the Clickbank Shopping center. A way which the Clickbank Mall is so gratifying is it may well operate a method to centralize working with some robust Environment-extensive-World-wide-web advertising and internet marketing instruments that Clickbank can make offered. Once you create a Clickbank Industry, you could supply website owners which has a free of charge Clickbank search box that may produce prospects right to your mall to assist make purchases. Then Any time a shopper can take advantage of that lookup box, you attain a Rate in addition to your present-day Clickbank Fee just like a direct Clickbank affiliate. It is really One more layer of profitability in your case. In combination with these Benefits, Clickbank has an promotion technique that actually functions very similar to the Google Adsense approach nonetheless it definitely way more lucrative as it truly is skilled at the Clickbank affiliate workforce and boosting your profitability, which naturally would make them combined with the shops on Clickbank way more worthwhile also. It is possible to make the most of the Clickbank Advertisements absolutely cost-free and so they greater however than Adsense as you receive a Rate with the sale rather then just by the press so your consider for each sale is way higher when compared towards the quite little quantities pay back back per click can supply. The wonderful thing about the Clickbank shopping mall is that after you transfer by way of all the procedure of making your very own thoroughly absolutely free shopping mall, it critically will turn out to be your advertising and marketing and advertising and marketing presence which you could use as your comprehensive entrance cease on your affiliate corporation. In laymen's problems Meaning that if you have been looking to get a way for making some huge funds by way of Net advertising and marketing implementing affiliate profits even so , you don't want the overhead and fuss of your personal private Internet site with many of the cost and complicated work that usually usually takes, the Clickbank Mall is a perfect Alternative. You might not surprisingly utilize your present Entire world-broad-Net house and develop the advertising and marketing worth Along with the look for bar and backlinks which can make the Clickbank Shopping mall carry out basically as An extra Site of 1's Website. But When you've got been endeavoring to get into Entire world-large-World-wide-web promoting and promoting in a major way with no stress of the online market place site, This is really The perfect Choice for You In addition mght. The Clickbank Shopping mall will crank out a fully useful Sector Web site that can provide the front end on your income and supply considerable volumes of Clickbank money but nevertheless be introduced in direction of your clientele as your Web page as well as your Current market. When you start to get shifting employing this amazing attribute of Clickbank, The cash producing capabilities that continue being to find out will go on to impact you this is a terrific way to go. And the more you exploit this supply, the extra money you make by yourself as well as your companions. That is why This is usually these kinds of a fantastic Source that Clickbank materials to its affiliates.

1.000.000$ WITH GOOGLE IN SIX MONTHS

Have been you mindful? That World wide web promoting revenues attained an believed new document of $4.two billion Together with the 3rd quarter of 2006 Which the Internet internet marketing market has been developing a lot more than thirty% for the last four consecutive numerous several years. "Google described revenues of $a few.sixty six billion for that quarter completed March 31, 2007" Google Adsense is revolutionizing the net, highschool Youthful youngsters are producing fortunes for each 30 times with Adsense needing to pay out their courses and serving to their fathers paying the fees in your own home. Legal professionals and Health-related practitioners gaved up their procedures to make hundreds of thousands with Google. Owing to Google Adsense revenues the net market put is growing quite a bit more quickly each day, when Google is paying out the expenses Site proprietors create further superior-quality World wide web web-sites with free facts and utilities for everybody, Sites that you search for when your hard money movement is fading. Folks Establish Internet web-sites only for get paid income with Adsense which bring about is reflecting over the internet contributing in direction of the speedy progress of Many Worldwide-web-web pages and principles that born every single day. If you use Adwords to promote your merchandise that you are sponsoring and broughting to Life style a fresh star mounting

Net-site which might be a necessity benefit to the online. This is precisely why Google Adsense/Adwords plans are so great, simply because The majority of people wins, advertisers spend for every click on and make income making use of Adwords, clicks and impressions are designed via the Adsense publishers that acquire payment, It is just a rollercoster that in no way stops so hence it is actually unbeatable. It is actually named "money sharing" and It really is One of the more powerfull Online promoting and advertising Software program you may at any time learn! An enormous quantity of people on a daily basis discover Adsense and start setting up hard cash at the house with their Net internet sites, they share The trick with Folks and when Some Other people gain funds Each human being could make funds, This is why I had The difficulty to jot down and distribute this minimal submitting, to spread The wonderful information and off monitor make my own fortune. When you've got an internet web site and are looking for a substantial income This may be the top chance so that you could get, Adsense is the greatest pounds creating plan circulating on the web, One of the a lot more properly compensated out Otherwise the number 1 and Additionally it could be genuine! Be Section of Google Adsense Totally absolutely free and retire from a posture in months, use Google Adwords to stand up your smaller business enterprise and become a millionaire in the following calendar year. Enable me to let you know with regards to the headline one.000.000 in 6 months: In addition to the Adsense earnings and Adwords web site readers that you could crank out It's also probable to produce large revenue referring Other people about the Adwords and Adsense methods, when they make full use of the packages you receives a commission, properly compensated. This seriously is how the plans execute, by have Google textual content content: "When an advertiser who signed up for Google AdWords as a result of your referral spends $5.00 (Along with the $5.00 indicator-up rate) inside of 90 situations of signal-up, you could be credited with $5.00. When that exact same advertiser spends $100.00 inside of just ninety days of indicator-up, you're going to be credited with an additional $40.00. If, in Just about any 100 and eighty-Performing day time period, you refer twenty advertisers who Every unique shell out about $a hundred.00 inside of ninety days in their respective indication-ups, you'll turn out awarded a $600.00 reward." "Every time a publisher who signed up for Google AdSense by your referral earns $5.00 within a person hundred eighty times of indication-up, you are going to be credited with $five.00. When that very same publisher earns $one hundred.00 in just only one hundred eighty days of indicator-up which happens to be appropriate for payout, you'll be credited with yet another $250.00. If, in almost any one hundred eighty working day interval, you refer 25 publishers who each achieve better than $100.00 and as a consequence are all eligible for payout, you may well be awarded a $two,000.00 reward." Do I really need to say the rest to affect you to enroll? I Don't Visualize so. Just do The maths and you will see out the potential of 1's earnings, must you by now know the techniques you understand what im Talking about and also have a considerably improved standpoint, If you don't I show you this, you'll be able to glimpse but I promise that does not exist Completely nothing at all else like it. And do not fret, just consider it simple, pick your effort and time, it is not likely to subject if you do not fully grasp any of this, the one situation is there is a Web page and intend to generate profits with it, in the process you are going to discover how Pretty much everything is efficient And just how tho accomplish your targets. And that is for this and all types of other things that Google is and will be the internet's No 1 for quite some time to come! Adhere to the path, come to be wealthy and make your goals show up true once and for all!!

3 VITAL EQUIPMENT FOR YOUR AFFILIATE MARKETER

Are you presently presently Completely ready to determine the solutions you've now been on the lookout for? Just what exactly does it should need to be a prosperous Affiliate Marketer? What exactly are the components of an affiliate advertising and marketing and advertising and marketing good results story? Is there a shortcut to Affiliate Promoting glory? Each one of those feelings Engage in about whilst inside the minds of affiliate Business owners who intend to really make it enormous Within this put. Even so affiliate promotion is touted as One of the very best and uttermost effective means to build hard cash online, It's not as simple as it Appears. The wise affiliate marketer types Just about every person go and executes it the simplest way he can. He also needs to raise the probable to understand good results by using the correct instruments suited to A prosperous Affiliate Marketing approach. We now have consulted most of pretty probably the best affiliate Business owners while in the location and reduce down are the very best three crucial methods for virtually any flourishing affiliate advertising tiny organization.

Critical Strategies #1:

Your very own personal World wide web-web page The ideal significant and indispensable Software program in Affiliate Advertising is your own Internet site. The Main motion in almost any flourishing affiliate promoting and advertising and marketing Firm is creating a great, plausible and Specialist searching Web site. Your website could be the bounce off posture of your entire marketing and advertising initiatives. As a result, It can be essential to Preliminary generate an -easy-to-use Web site, which could appeal to your future prospective buyers and stimulate them to click the hyperlinks to the goods and remedies you are marketing and Optimistically , develop a get. For that rationale, you might want to at first focus your endeavours in developing a web site which might cater to what your prospects have to have.An extremely strong thing you ought to consider is that just about all Net individuals go online to look for specifics, not quickly to go and purchase one thing. Previously mentioned all else, make your website full of exclusive, pertinent and realistic written content. People today now adore material content articles which may be exciting and valuable. Take into account that, in The online, substance is always very important and greatest significant-high quality information would not just increase your trustworthiness, it may help you to definitely fulfil a far better-volume online online search engine score. By publishing pertinent and helpful content articles, you create your self as being a reputable authority within the sphere, exhibiting you a genuine endorser to the products and solutions or services you support. Establishing a very good standing is a great go in building up a devoted customer foundation.

Critical Strategies #2:

Incentives Competition is extremely fierce from the Internet whole earth. You need to continually be only one-motion beforehand of one's rivals in order that you just seize a substantial share within your target marketplace place. So, you should use Each and every conceivable usually means to inspire people now not exclusively to go to your web site and also to easily click on and begin for the net-web sites on the choices and qualified companies you might be endorsing. Developing an choose-in electronic mail listing is Among the many enhanced procedures to collect potential prospects. Give a publication or an e-zine. Improved but, provide incentives with your prospective customers to inspire them to subscribe as part of your newsletters. You could possibly existing gratis softwares, entry to exceptional companies and numerous freebies That could be helpful towards the prospective customers.

Critical Strategies #3: Url Attractiveness

The value of driving remarkably targeted visitors to your Net website can not be emphasized a lot of. The all-critical Web-site focused website visitors is on the best with the listing of possibly The key entities in the world wide web arena. Attracting people now to your site has acquired to be the key motion you'll want to carry out. Do every single minimal detail to attain An important search engine placement. Backlink Attractiveness is Among the many aspects that engines like google like google use to ascertain Net online search engine rankings. so, to elevate your connection popularity, you will have to start an intensive reciprocal backlink motion. Deemed amongst the greater usually means To try this, at no cost in the slightest degree, is by distributing posting articles, using your Internet site's World-wide-web tackle Within the source box, to e-zines and free report internet sites. You may not only get publicity, You might also have the chance to promote for free of charge, just include things like such things as a hyperlink pointing to your site. The greater Internet websites you deliver your content material content to, the higher your internet site website link attractiveness is. Be specified your posting written content are distinctive, pertinent and realistic to make sure that other Web sites may well make your mind up it up and publish it. They're absolutely but three of the different tools that an affiliate marketer can use to produce up earning possible. The probabilities are infinite and they're restricted only by your eyesight, creativeness, resourcefulness and backbone. It is achievable to usually have a look at other Strategies and adapt other methods, which you suspect could perhaps allow it to be easier to grow to be a considerable rolling affiliate marketer. Many thanks for finding the time to review my limited posting. You might want to go on looking For added info to assist you. Affiliate Marketing inside the Nutshell Just what is affiliate marketing and advertising and advertising and marketing? Affiliate advertising and marketing is The one quickest growth field on the web. It's also accurate that affiliate advertising and marketing and marketing and advertising is most likely the quickest and many Resourceful strategies to receive income and also have a occupation on the internet. To put it simply, affiliate marketing is promoting products and solutions and remedies on the Charge basis. You possess a business that advertises and sells items for other businesses. You could have an merchandise of your own personal private to begin with or not. The things that An effective affiliate marketer require to have are: one.Your internet site is unquestionably the jumping off position of your advertising and marketing and advertising initiatives. Hence the Preliminary phase in almost any successful affiliate marketing small business is building a wonderful, credible and Capable looking Web page. You need to establish a person-valuable Web content, that may entice your possible clientele and inspire them to click on the backlinks towards your expert services and items you'll be endorsing and make a invest in. You'll find corporations whose organization is setting up World-wide-web internet sites you could possibly use to construct one for yourself.

You should discover merchandise to provide, you will need to have the opportunity to ascertain regardless of no matter if There exists a desire for anybody products and solutions and if Gentlemen and women will truly put money into them. You might either have your individual Main merchandise or things which are created by Other individuals. Which ever way you go, It is necessary to believe in the goods. a few.Will probably be essential for you to become an adept advertiser and regulate to inform if the promotion you are paying for is generating added cash flow on your own in comparison to the marketing is costing you. four.It's important that you have fantastic mathematical abilities. You should handle to monitor your gross profits and determine profits, in addition to, see to it that your suppliers are paid in full and promptly. 5.You'll have the whole and unwavering guidance of All of your family members so you could dedicate the time and Vitality important to commence your affiliate promoting and advertising Firm. Pinpointing an Current Sizzling Have to have Each compact organization owner acknowledges that Opponents is tough, but they won't be effective at pinpoint specifically what adjustments are wished-for as being a method of getting to the highest. Conducting little small business as standard may no more be enough. Getting the technological know-how that is definitely now made available may be really a terrific enable or probably a financial establishment breaker. Plainly most small tiny business enterprise and household primarily based company are the two starving (they don't have a lot more than enough technological know-how) or They may be obese (they have every thing piece of new technological innovation that arrives down the pike). There exists, nonetheless, some relatively new techno- logical innovation that each tiny or Residence dependent enter- prise proprietor involves. It may respond to ideas like; how can modest firms detect noteworthy tendencies, Establish an exist- ing sizzling want and make much better choices more rapidly? Respond to: small business intelligence program. Company intel- ligence will be the crystal ball within the 20 initially century. Obtaining modest enterprise intelligence (BI) computer software package deal is Among the many most strategic investments that a business may possibly make. Utilizing specifics mining, report- ing and querying, BI aids enterprises have an understanding of, keep an eye on, regulate and respond to specified circumstances. This Pc software package empowers resolve-makers — and staff members customers — to attach the dots around very important compact small business portions in a means Earlier unimagin- able. BI aids you decide: ·Which buyers are fulfilling? ·Which con- sumers show up valuable but generally usually are not? ·Are you close as much as — or Significantly from — accomplishing vital milestones? ·When is the best the proper time for you to start a advertising and marketing internet marketing campaign? ·What was one of the most useful carrying out products or services ultimate quarter? Compact business Intelligence application might be quite a bit far more of an money commitment than modest firms can bear. It could quite possibly definitely be pricy. Minimal modest organization or dwelling business people, even so, can subscribe to BI answers on the web at a reasonably cost-effective Value. You'll find numerous to select from. eBay also posted a "Unbelievably warm Objects" checklist the 1st week of each month. It offers critical facts and info to eBay sellers who use fall shippers. Safeguarding your Commissions Burglars undoubtedly are a problem out Within the brick and mortar surroundings is for entrepreneurs and robbers are a priority for cyber Place business people. Out with the brick and mortar total entire world, thieves will pick revenue and items and it isn't any exclusive on the internet. The legitimate whole environment merchants use locks and alarms to prevent robbers. World-wide-web business people need to use anti-theft Laptop or computer software package to defend their commissions. Allow me to share numerous things you are able to do to safeguard oneself furthermore your commissions: one.Use Meta Refresh: A meta refresh is a straightforward little bit of HTML code which mechanically redirects your customer to another webpage (your affiliate URL). It offers a neat indicates of presenting affiliate inbound links in newsletters. It most certainly assists lower Fee bypassing and commission hijacking. A giant advantage of making use of meta refreshes is the fact if merchants enhance their affiliate inbound backlinks, you'll transform hyperlinks on dozens of Web content rapidly and easily by altering just one file. An individual difficulty is the fact that some search engines like google and yahoo don't like meta refreshes just because They are routinely helpful for unsavory makes use of. Consequently if you make use of This method, benefit from it with warning. two.Use a URL redirection provider. You can use Certainly free of charge services or invest in a unique domain detect for every affiliate system you be Portion of. URL redirection will make affiliate inbound hyperlinks less noticeable, so this will likely Lower down some Payment thefts. three.Use an internet-centered advertisement monitoring assistance. The advert monitoring backlink in the beginning hides the affiliate hyperlink, lessening thefts. four.Use an advert monitoring script. Terrific advert monitoring scripts disguise the affiliate url along with acquiring valuable for monitoring. It really is bought the edge that it is not going to boost A few other human being's region. five.Use JavaScript redirect. Since this initially hides the affiliate connection, it need to definitely cut down Payment thefts. Remember that thievery is a challenge for on the web corporations and acquire the necessary steps to shield your commissions.

UTILIZE A MAILING LIST OF YOUR OWN

What ever type of electronic mail you deliver out, you'll require a mailing checklist. The essential way to make a mailing checklist is by capturing determine and e mail handle facts for everyone who purchases or displays curiosity inside your products or services. An Digital mail listing that you simply Accumulate You is truly worth its system excess weight in gold. This may be attained by using a listing supervisor on your web site. Listing professionals also give the HTML coding for the form on the Gateway Online internet pages. A listing supervisor collects the e-mail addresses which are collected With all the kind. As a result, your electronic mail listing is gathered. This could get some time so there are actually strategies to use right until you can get the really possess e-mail listing built. A method to establish a mailing listing is usually to perform advertisement swaps with other history entrepreneurs. The way where this performs is, you (as organization A) have an e-mail history you deliver out newsletters to and A further checklist operator (firm B) has a list they send out newsletters to. Enterprise A and Corporation B position adverts on one another's mailing lists. Every single of you is advertising Yet another's listing. You will be able to lease or get experienced e-mail lists. The listing you establish utilizing your have consumers' names is named your "house listing." Certainly, everytime you're pretty 1st getting started, your own residence list is probably going to normally be skimpy. To reinforce it, one particular system to go is rent or purchase a mailing record. You'll find two techniques to acquire or lease a mailing document—approaching the organization you would like to lease from quickly or making use of a listing broker. Any Firm that email messages information and facts and points to its purchasers ordinarily incorporates a listing manager, who handles inquiries and orders with the mailing listing. One more method to establish an e-mail checklist is usually to checklist your publication in the entire ezine directories.

ABOUT THE AUTHOR

TOM JACKSON is a newcomer on Amazon and he wants to give you a series on how to make money online. Tom already succeeded in this area and is an expert in making money online. So he will show you also how to accomplish this. He lives in Kapaa, Hawaii with his fiancé. Tom loves educating and inspiring other authors and entrepreneurs to succeed and live the life of their dreams.

OTHER BOOKS BY TOM CORSON-KNOWLES

TBA

One Last Thing...

If you enjoyed this book or found it useful I'd be very grateful if you'd post a short review on Amazon. Your support really does make a difference and I read all the reviews personally so I can get your feedback and make this book even better.

If you'd like to leave a review then all you need to do is click the review link on this book's page on Amazon.

Thanks again for your support!